Jungle Animals

By Ruth Owen

WINDMILL BOOKS

New York

Published in 2015 by Windmill Books, An Imprint of Rosen Publishing
29 East 21st Street, New York, NY 10010

First Edition

Produced for Rosen by Ruby Tuesday Books Ltd
Editor for Ruby Tuesday Books Ltd: Mark J. Sachner
Designer: Emma Randall

Photo Credits:
Cover, 1, 3, 5, 6–7, 8–9, 10–11, 12–13, 14–15, 16–17, 18–19, 20–21, 22–23, 24–25, 26–27, 28–29, 31 © Ruby Tuesday Books; cover, 4–5, 6, 10, 14, 18, 22, 26 © Shutterstock.

Library of Congress Cataloging-in-Publication Data

Owen, Ruth, 1967– author.
 Jungle animals / by Ruth Owen. — First Edition.
    pages cm. — (Origami safari)
 Includes index.
 ISBN 978-1-4777-9238-4 (library binding) —
ISBN 978-1-4777-9239-1 (pbk.) — ISBN 978-1-4777-9240-7 (6-pack)
1. Origami—Juvenile literature. 2. Jungle animals in art—Juvenile literature. 3. Animals in art—Juvenile literature. I. Title.
 TT872.5.O935 2015
 736.982—dc23
                                    2014013974

Manufactured in the United States of America

CPSIA Compliance Information: Batch #WS14PK8: For Further Information contact Rosen Publishing, New York, New York at 1-800-237-9932

Contents

Jungle Origami

Jungles are hot, rainy **habitats** where lots of trees and other plants grow. In fact, there are so many plants growing close together in a jungle that they tangle together.

Many **rain forests** have areas of thick jungle that are home to thousands of different types of **mammals**, birds, **reptiles**, **insects**, and spiders.

In this book you can find out about the lives of six animals that live in jungles and rain forests. You will also get the chance to make a cool model of each animal using **origami**, which is the ancient art of folding paper.

All you need is some colorful, square paper, and you will be ready to make your own collection of origami jungle animals.

An orangutan in a jungle

Origami Orangutan

Orangutans live high in rain forest trees, up to 100 feet (30.5 m) above the ground. They are the largest tree-living animals on Earth. Orangutans live on the islands of Borneo and Sumatra in Southeast Asia.

Adult orangutans usually live alone. They spend their days climbing and swinging through the treetops looking for food. Orangutans eat about 300 different types of fruit. They also eat other parts of plants, mushrooms, insects, spiders, and eggs.

An adult male orangutan tries to become the boss of an area in the forest. He then gets to mate with the females in that area. He makes loud calls and grows large cheek pads that show other males he's in charge!

YOU WILL NEED:

- To make an orangutan, one sheet of orange paper
- Scissors • A marker

Step 1:

Place the paper colored side down. Fold in half, and crease.

Fold in half again, and crease.

Step 2:

Now open up the top layer of paper to create a pocket.

Pocket

Gently squash down the pocket to form a square.

Step 3:

Turn the model over. Open out the triangle-shaped section of the model to create a pocket.

Open out here

Gently squash down the pocket to form a square.

Step 4:

Fold in the left- and right-hand sides of the model along the dotted lines, and crease. You should only be folding the top layer of paper.

Step 5:

Fold down the top point of the model, and crease.

Top point

Top point

Step 6:

Now open out the folds you made in steps 4 and 5 to create a pocket.

Pocket

Hold onto the top point of the pocket and pull it backward while gently squashing and flattening the sides of the pocket inward to create a diamond shape.

Step 7:

Turn the model over. Fold in both side points, and crease well. Then fold down the small triangular flap in the center of the model.

Next, open out the three folds you've just made to create a pocket (as you did in step 6). Take the top point of the pocket and pull it backward while gently squashing and flattening the sides of the pocket to create a diamond shape.

Your model should now look like this.

Step 8:

Fold the two side points of the model into the center along the dotted lines. You should only be folding the top layer of paper.

Step 9:

Turn the model over and repeat step 8. Then rotate the model 180 degrees.

Your model should now look like this.

Step 10:

To make the orangutan's head, fold up the bottom flap of the model. Cut off the pointed end of the flap along the dotted line. Then fold any edges of the flap behind to create the orangutan's forehead.

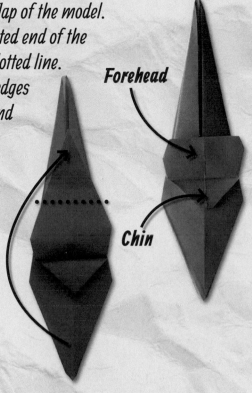

Forehead

Chin

Step 11:

To make the orangutan's arms, fold over one of the top points and crease hard. Then unfold, open out the arm, and fold it inside out using the crease you've just made. Fold the tip of the arm to make a hand.

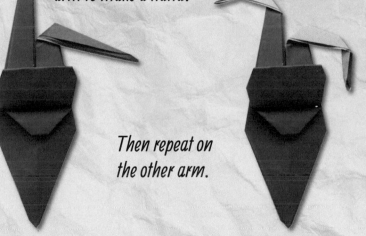

Then repeat on the other arm.

Step 12:

To make the orangutan's legs, make a short cut up the bottom point of the model. Fold the two points outward to create the orangutan's feet.

Step 13:

Draw the orangutan's face with a marker.

Origami Parrot

There are around 350 different **species**, or types, of parrots. Most types of wild parrots live in the trees in jungle areas and rain forests

Often, parrots live in large groups called flocks. Most parrots find a **mate** and stay with that partner for life. Parrots do not build nests, but they use holes in old trees as a safe place to lay their eggs. Sometimes parrots use holes in cliffs or banks of soil as a nest.

Parrots feed on foods such as seeds, fruit, buds, **pollen** and **nectar** from flowers, and sometimes insects.

Large parrots, such as macaws, can live as long as a human—up to 80 years and sometimes longer!

Step 1:

Place the paper colored side down. Fold the paper in half, crease well, and then unfold. Fold the paper in half again, in the opposite direction, crease well, and then unfold.

Step 2:

Fold the top and bottom points into the center crease along the dotted lines. Crease well, and then unfold.

Step 3:

Now fold the top and bottom points into the center crease in the opposite direction. Crease well, and then unfold.

Beak-like pocket

Step 4:

Now gently fold the top half of the paper into the center crease while allowing the top point to create a beak-like pocket. Then squash the pocket and fold it to the right-hand side of the model.

Squashed beak-like pocket

Center crease

Repeat on the bottom half of the model.

Step 5:

Turn the model over. Fold down the top half along the center crease.

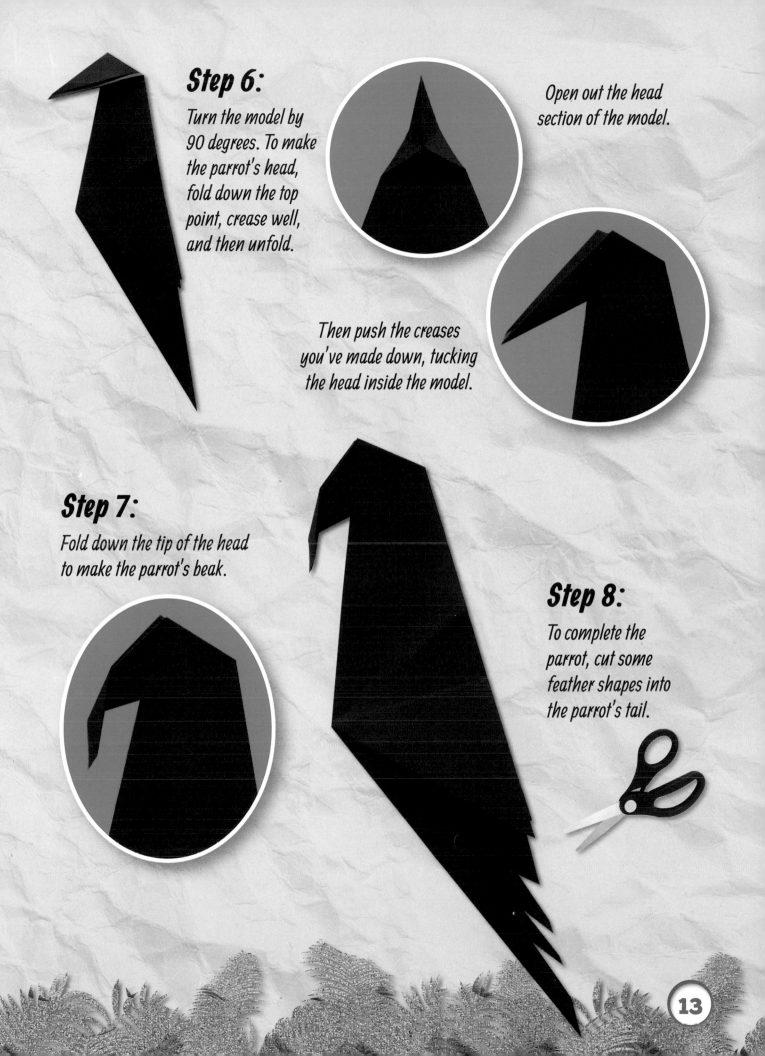

Step 6:

Turn the model by 90 degrees. To make the parrot's head, fold down the top point, crease well, and then unfold.

Open out the head section of the model.

Then push the creases you've made down, tucking the head inside the model.

Step 7:

Fold down the tip of the head to make the parrot's beak.

Step 8:

To complete the parrot, cut some feather shapes into the parrot's tail.

Origami Snake

Many different species of snakes make their homes in the tangled branches of jungle trees.

Green tree pythons are long snakes that live in rain forests in New Guinea and Australia. They can grow to be about five feet (1.5 m) long.

A green tree python hunts at night. It wraps its tail tightly around a branch, then waits for a bird, frog, lizard, or rat to pass by. The python grabs its **prey** with its mouth. Then the snake kills its victim by squeezing it to death with its body. Finally, the snake swallows the animal whole. After a meal of tasty rat, this jungle hunter may not eat again for up to two weeks!

YOU WILL NEED:

- To make a snake, one sheet of paper that's green on both sides

Step 1:

Fold the paper in half, crease, and then unfold.

Fold the top and bottom points into the center crease to create a kite shape. Crease well.

Step 2:

Fold the top and bottom points into the center crease again, along the dotted lines, to create a thinner kite shape. Crease well.

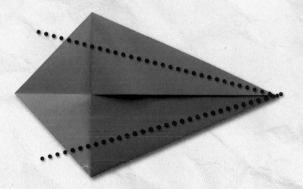

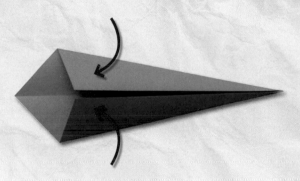

Step 3:

One last time, fold the top and bottom points of the model into the center, and crease well.

15

Step 4:

Fold the model in half so that the center crease is at the top of the model.

Step 5:

To make the head end of the snake, fold up the left-hand end of the model. Crease hard, and unfold.

Step 6:

Open out the left-hand end of the model, and using the crease you just made, fold the end of the model backward, so it closes around the snake's body.

Step 7:

Fold down the head end of the model, crease well, and unfold.

Now, open out the head.

Using the crease you just made, fold the tip of the head forward and close up the head.

Step8:

Now fold down the right-hand end of the model.
Crease hard, and unfold.

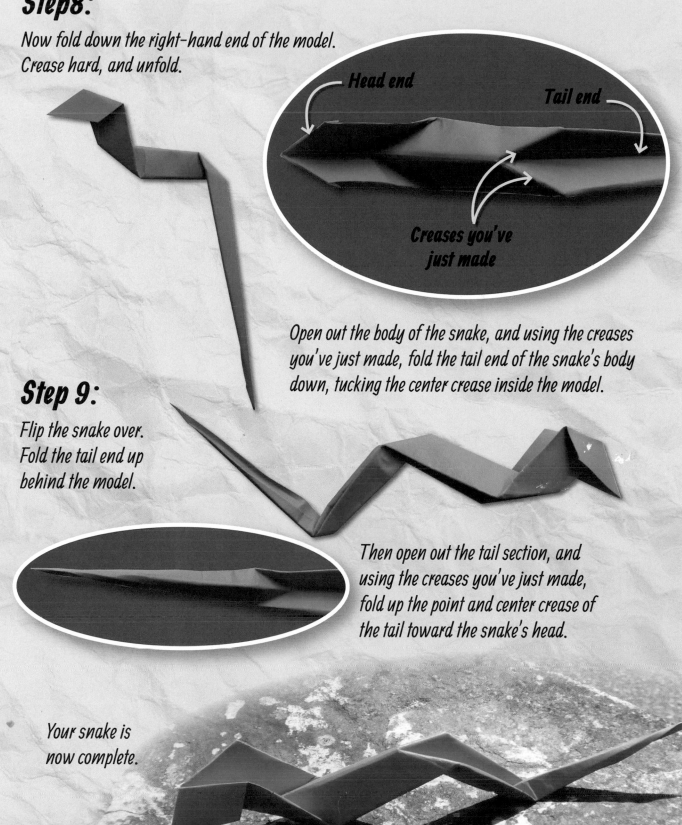

Head end

Tail end

Creases you've
just made

Open out the body of the snake, and using the creases
you've just made, fold the tail end of the snake's body
down, tucking the center crease inside the model.

Step 9:

Flip the snake over.
Fold the tail end up
behind the model.

Then open out the tail section, and
using the creases you've just made,
fold up the point and center crease of
the tail toward the snake's head.

Your snake is
now complete.

Origami Chameleon

Chameleons are colorful reptiles. There are over 150 different species of these lizards. Many types of chameleons live in trees in rain forests.

Chameleons are able to make their skin color brighter or darker. They are also able to change their skin color. They do this to **communicate** with other chameleons. A chameleon might change its color to show it is afraid or angry.

When it is time to mate, males brighten their colors to become more attractive to female chameleons. Females can even change color to let male chameleons know they are pregnant and do not want to be bothered!

Step 1:

Fold the paper in half, crease, and then unfold. Next, fold each half into the center, and crease well.

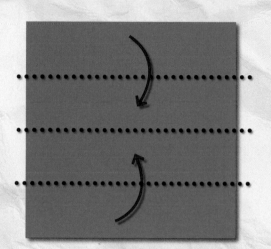

Step 2:

Now fold the sides of the model into the center to make a square, crease well, and then unfold both sides.

Step 3:

Now lift up the top left-hand corner of the model to create a pocket. Using the creases you made in steps 1 and 2, gently squeeze and flatten the pocket to make a triangle.

Pocket

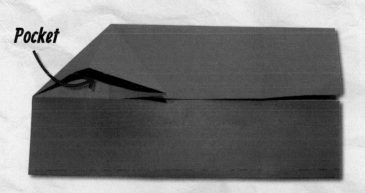

Step 4:

Repeat step 3 on the other three corners of the model.

Triangle

Step 5:

Turn the model over. Fold the top right-hand and bottom right-hand points into the center crease, and crease well.

Repeat on the left-hand side to make a diamond shape. Then fold up the bottom half of the model.

Your model should now look like this.

Step 6:

Make the chameleon's legs by folding out the two small triangles on each side of the model.

Step 7:

To make the chameleon's head, fold back one of the end points of the model so that it touches a leg. Crease well and then unfold.

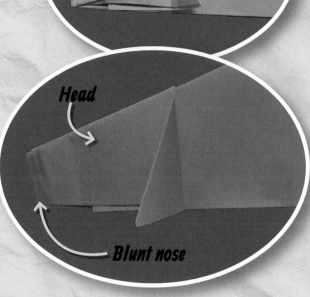

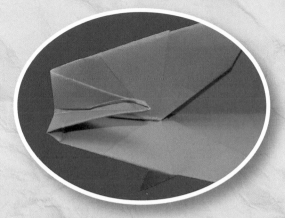

Open out the head end of the model, and using the creases you've just made, fold the point back into the head to give the chameleon a blunt nose. Then close up the head.

Step 8:

To make the chameleon's tail, fold down the tail end of the model, crease well, and then unfold.

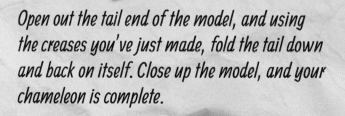

Open out the tail end of the model, and using the creases you've just made, fold the tail down and back on itself. Close up the model, and your chameleon is complete.

Opened out tail folding back on itself

Origami Frog

There are many different frog species living in the world's jungles. In fact, there are more than 1,000 different types of frogs living in just the Amazon rain forest in South America! Some of the world's jungle frogs are highly dangerous.

The golden poison dart frog is only 1 inch (2.5 cm) long, but it is one of the most poisonous animals on Earth. This tiny **amphibian** produces a powerful poison in its skin. If a person touches the frog's skin, the poison can enter his or her body through a cut or scratch. Just a tiny amount of poison from a touch can be enough to kill a person!

Step 1:

Place the paper colored side down, fold in half, and crease.

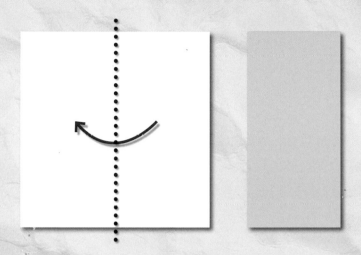

Step 2:

Fold over the top left-hand corner of the model, crease, and then unfold. Repeat on the top right-hand corner.

Step 3:

Now fold over the top of the model. You should fold at the place where the creases you made in step 2 meet. Then unfold.

Step 4:

Take the two sides of the model and begin to squash them into the center. As you do this, the creases you've made will make the top of the model collapse into a triangle.

Step 5:

To make the frog's front legs, fold up the two bottom points of the triangle along the dotted lines, and crease hard.

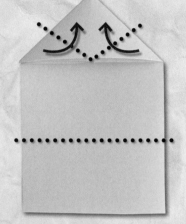

Then fold up the bottom half of the model, and crease.

Step 6:

Now fold in the sides of the model so that they meet in the center. Crease hard.

Step 7:

Fold up the bottom of the model, and crease hard. Now open out the bottom of the model to make a pocket. Squash down and flatten the pocket against the model.

Pocket

Flattened Pocket

Step 8:

Next, open out one of the side pockets at the bottom of the model. Then squash and flatten it down to create a point. Repeat on the other side.

Then fold back each point to create the frog's back legs.

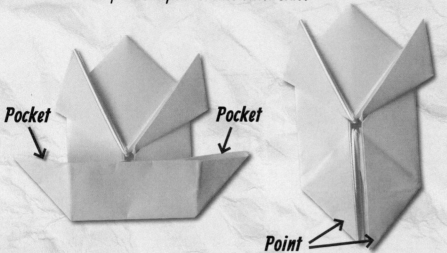

Pocket

Pocket

Point

Step 9:

Fold up the bottom of the model, and crease hard. Then fold it back down again, making a small pleat.

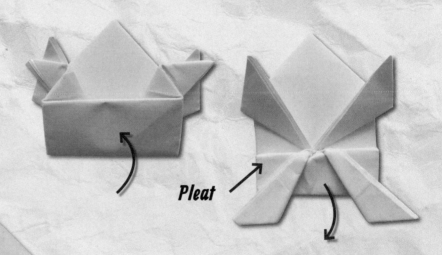

Pleat

Flip the model over and your frog is complete.

Pleat

Origami Butterfly

Hundreds of thousands of different species of insects live in jungles and rain forests. This number includes many types of butterflies.

One of the largest butterflies in the world, the blue morpho, is found in forests in Mexico, and parts of Central and South America. The wings of this butterfly can grow to be 8 inches (20 cm) across. When folded, with the underside showing, the butterfly's wings are a dull brown. When fully opened, the bright blue upper surface can be seen.

Blue morphos feed on tree **sap** and juices from rotting fruit and fungi. They also feed on liquids from the rotting bodies of dead animals. The butterflies suck up these liquids through a long, straw-like mouthpart called a proboscis.

Step 1:

Place the paper colored side down, fold in half from side to side, crease, and unfold. Then fold down from top to bottom, crease, and unfold.

Step 2:

Now fold the four points into the center of the model, and crease well.

Step 3:

Turn the model over. Now fold all four points into the center, and crease hard.

Step 4:

Unfold all the folds you've just made. Your piece of paper should look like this.

Step 5:

Now fold in the two sides of the paper so that they meet in the center, and crease.

Step 6:

Unfold and open out the top half of the model. Then using the creases you made in the earlier stages, gently squash and flatten the top of the model.

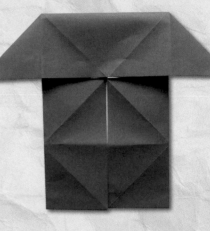

Step 7:

Repeat step 6 on the bottom half of the model.

Step 8:

Fold the model in half so that the open sections are at the top.

Step 9:

Take the model's top left-hand point, fold it down along the dotted line, and crease. Repeat with the top right-hand point. You should only be folding down the top layer of paper.

Step 10:

Make a small fold along the dotted lines on each side of the model. Crease well.

Step 11:

Now fold the model in half along its center.

Fold over the top right-hand edge of the model along the dotted line, and crease hard. Then unfold.

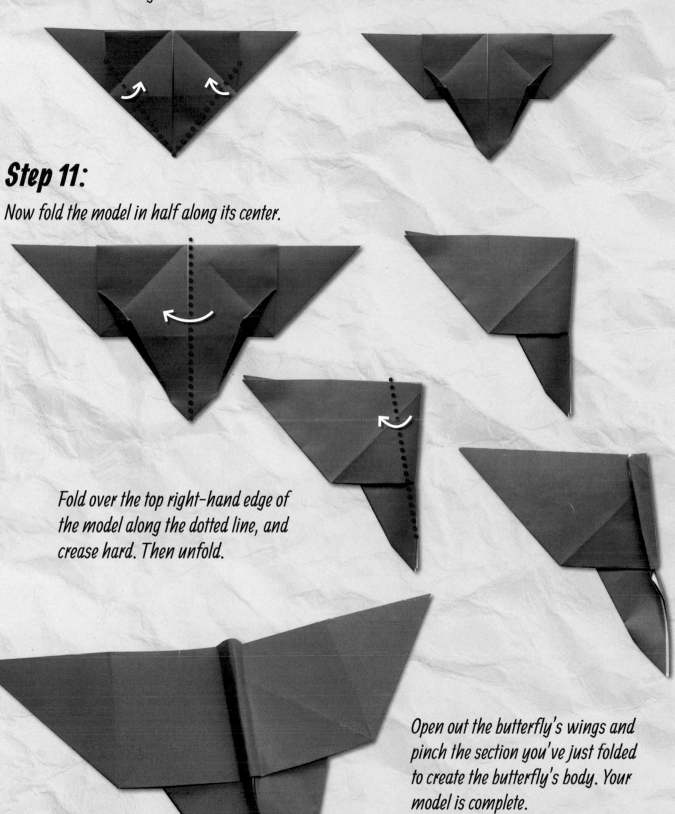

Open out the butterfly's wings and pinch the section you've just folded to create the butterfly's body. Your model is complete.

Glossary

amphibian (am-FIB-ee-un)
A cold-blooded animal such as a frog, toad, or salamander. Most amphibians begin their lives in water as larvae that breathe underwater through gills. As adults, amphibians live on land and breathe air with lungs.

communicate
(kuh-MYOO-nih-kayt)
To share facts or feelings.

habitats (HA-buh-tats)
Places where animals or plants normally live. A habitat may be a jungle, a grassland, the ocean, or a backyard.

insects (IN-sekts)
Small animals that have a hard covering called an exoskeleton, six legs, two antennae, and a body in three sections.

jungles (JUNG-gulz)
Hot, often very wet, habitats where so many trees and plants grow close together that they become tangled.

mammals (MA-mulz)
Warm-blooded animals that have backbones and usually have hair, breathe air, and feed milk to their young.

mate (MAYT)
When a male and a female animal get together to produce young.

nectar (NEK-tur)
A sweet liquid, produced by flowers, that many insects and other animals eat.

origami (or-uh-GAH-mee)
The art of folding paper to make small models. Origami has been popular in Japan for hundreds of years. It gets its name from the Japanese words *ori*, which means "folding," and *kami*, which means "paper."

pollen (PAH-lin)
A colored dust made on the anthers of flowers, which plants need in order to reproduce.

prey (PRAY)
An animal that is hunted by another animal as food.

rain forests (RAYN FOR-ests)
Warm, wooded habitats with a lot of rainfall and many types of animals and plants.

reptiles (REP-tylz)
Animals such as snakes, lizards, turtles, crocodiles, and alligators that are cold-blooded and have scaly skin.

sap (SAP)
A liquid that flows through plants carrying water and food.

species (SPEE-sheez)
One type of living thing. The members of a species look alike and can produce young together.

For web resources related to the subject of this book, go to:
www.windmillbooks.com/weblinks
and select this book's title.

Read More

Allgor, Marie. *Endangered Rainforest Animals.* Save Earth's Animals. New York: PowerKids Press, 2013.

Berne, Emma Carlson. *Chameleons: Masters of Disguise!* Animal Superpowers. New York: PowerKids Press, 2013.

de Lambilly-Bresson, Elisabeth. *Animals in the Jungle.* Animal Show and Tell. New York: Gareth Stevens Publishing, 2008.

Index